Apocrypha

Apocrypha

David Southward

RESOURCE *Publications* · Eugene, Oregon

APOCRYPHA

Resource Publications
An Imprint of Wipf and Stock Publishers
199 W. 8th Ave., Suite 3
Eugene, OR 97401

www.wipfandstock.com

PAPERBACK ISBN: 978-1-5326-5256-1
HARDCOVER ISBN: 978-1-5326-5257-8
EBOOK ISBN: 978-1-5326-5258-5

Manufactured in the U.S.A.   06/08/18

. . . even though we once knew Christ from a human point of view, we know him no longer in that way.

(2 Cor 5:16, NRSV)

Contents

Acknowledgments

With gratitude to the editors of the journals in which the following poems first appeared:

The Other Journal: "The Cleansing of Mary Magdalene"

POEM: "A Neighbor's Concern" and "Joseph"

The St. Sebastian Review: "The Man Who Would Be King"

Verse-Virtual: "A Passover Supper" and "How He Came to Speak in Parables"

Annunciation

Crying herself to sleep, Mary dreamed
a man came calling with an angel's face.
He told her she was brimming with the grace
by which a world of sin could be redeemed.
So inconceivable did her fortune seem,
she questioned if the stranger's words were true.
He whispered soothingly, *The Lord is with you.*

She woke—and her imagination teemed
with confidence, now she'd been shown the way
to fend off any charge of indecorum.
She raced to Joseph's workshop, to relay
the destiny their Lord had chosen for him.
There'd be no need for guile or dropping clues;
she knew exactly how to break her news.

The Gift Bearers

Her newborn wailed from lying on rough hay
where migrants crowded, waiting to be registered.
She hoped they'd have the tact to look away—
till three magicians blurted that they'd heard
kings roar like him! They pulled out shiny globes
to catch his gaze, declared his birth a sign.
The incense of their gold-embroidered robes
transformed the crib into a makeshift shrine.
Even the shepherds leaned in to take part,
hailing the little conqueror of Rome.
His heavy lids were lifting Mary's heart
when Joseph returned; soon they could go home.
That night, as the child nursed in her soft sleeve,
she lulled him with the feats he would achieve.

A Passover Supper

His mother let him choose the yearling lamb.
Standing in line, waiting for Temple priests
to perform the sacrifice, his head swam
with spooling blood and clumps of matted fleece.

They dragged it home. He watched her drive a stave
across its shoulders, skewer down the spine
to hold it steady over coals—as she laved
the naked loin and ribs in a roasting brine.

Before the meal, his father told again
the story of Passover: how God spares
the chosen, how all Egypt is condemned.
He ate hastily, blinking back tears
which welled up from an unfamiliar tension.
A rush of kindness—mixed with apprehension.

Joseph

When the festival was ended and they started to return, the boy Jesus stayed behind in Jerusalem, but his parents did not know it.

(Luke 2:43, NRSV)

Three days we searched the city—called his name
through market stalls, down alleys, into wells.
I felt the hot fatigue of fear and blame
in Mary's tears. But how could I foretell
what he would do—this staid, abstracted boy
who memorized the prophets and withdrew
into himself? A childhood filled with joy
was brushed away like sawdust as he grew.

We found him in the Temple: all aglow
with rabbis' praise. They laughed that one so young
should ask of our concern, "Did you not know
I must be in my Father's house?" That stung
like nettles' fire. Anyone could see
the Father he referred to wasn't me.

Lacuna

She'd wash the frocks and watch her siblings play
echoing games, near to the spring-fed pool
where he would sometimes lead his father's mule
to drink. She talked to him. He liked the way
her stream of questions said, *You may, You may—*
letting the boy whose will was like a jewel
relax, enjoy himself, and be a fool.
The summer brought them close, until one day
she laid back and addressed him with a look
he could not meet.
              Seeing how he delayed,
she latched her hamper with a tenterhook
and led the children home from their charade.
He cursed himself. However long it took,
he'd find some reason for the rift he'd made.

A Neighbor's Concern

"Truly I tell you, no prophet is accepted in the prophet's hometown."
(Luke 4:24, NRSV)

He sleeps all day and roams the hills at night,
mumbling a psalm as though he chewed on bread—
then shuffles homeward through the morning light
with bloodshot eyes, like one already dead.
How can a full-grown man, at twenty-three,
not have a wife or steady occupation?
The village calls him Mary's Prodigy.
Our girls don't bother anymore to chase him:
he'd sooner kiss a beggar, court disease
beside a sickbed, or grow scarecrow thin
from wallowing in a state of vagrancy.
It's tragic, thinking what he might have been.
But mark my words: when Death knocks at his door,
he'll ask himself what he was living for.

He Hears of a Messiah

Word spread through Nazareth of a prophet, John,
who lived on locusts, preaching sin's remission
by water, on a healing expedition.
He sensed the rebel's faith, though frowned upon,
could waken interest in a world beyond
this world's mire—blending in one mission
the thrill of change and comfort of tradition.
John said a greater spokesman would go on
to signify the coming of the Lord,
one who would be more than an informant.
He could not still the resonating chord
within his breast, the wonder like a torment:
Is it I?—whose mere suggestion had restored
a dream too consequential to lie dormant.

John the Baptist

A crowd began to form, up on the bank
where a youth knelt loosening his sandals.
He chatted with the pilgrims at some length,
then draped his clothes across the purple thistle
and stepped into the Jordan. Straight for me
he waded, arms outstretched. The surface mist
dispersed—and everything I'd planned to say
was silenced by a look, brazen yet mild.
He filled his lungs with breath; the morning sky
grew clearer while I held him like a child
under the water. Washed in the full sun,
he came up dripping, gasped, shuddered and smiled
with surprise. I hardly knew what I had done.
It echoed through the valley: he was the one.

Satan in the Wilderness: Day Six

I find him sleeping, curled up in the shade
of tamarisks. The smell of wasting skin
tells me the pious hermit might be swayed,
now that starvation strains his discipline.
I blow against the damp nape of his neck.
His fingers twitch; he sits up, foggy-eyed.
Sensing my presence, he stiffens and draws back—
as though his own desires might be defied.
"If you are He," I say, "why be so soft?
Change these unwilling stones to loaves of bread."
"Man does not live by bread alone," he scoffs,
"but by the word that comes from the mouth of God."
How quaintly he mistakes his airs for graces—
and me for a mirage in an oasis.

Satan in the Wilderness: Day Twenty

I visit him every hour—a steady drum
of doubt against his sack of weakened bones.
He's sunk in some new phase (delirium?),
judging by telltale fractures in his tone.
His prayers sound meek; a simple wish to die
pokes through them like a truth through doublespeak.
It gives me an idea: to perch him high
above the earth, poised on the Temple's peak
where, if he fears to jump, I shall rebut
that angels' wings must catch the Lord's own calf.
He mutters, "It is written, 'Do not put
the Lord your God to the test.'" Well, that's a laugh!
What is this exile for, if not to test
His sovereignty and my relentlessness?

Satan in the Wilderness: Day Forty

I dangle empires—women, riches, fame—
before his glassy eyes. I share my cloak
of sable majesty, and set aflame
the night sky's opals for my masterstroke.
He studies me as through a puff of smoke
and answers in a whisper almost grim:
"Worship the Lord your God; serve only Him."
To think: the onslaught of my best techniques
against the soul of one iconoclast
should fizzle in a draw on this frontier!
But what's the use in arguing? He speaks
with such authority, it's clear
our period of rivalry has passed.
He knows that I am part of him at last.

Miracle at Cana

"But you have kept the good wine until now."
(John 2:10, NRSV)

His mother, seeing how anxiously the bride
gazed at the pitchers, whispered in his ear:
"They have no wine." He shrugged, grew more severe
and said, "My hour is not yet come." His pride
was purer than the flushed, anarchic tide
sweeping through men whose voices rose in cheer
when serving girls engaged a wolfish leer.
Why should such idle cups be fortified?
His mother fell silent. But her silence showed
how breaches between loved ones sometimes fill
with sympathy—as darkness fills with stars.
It touched him, so that when, turning to go,
she bid the kitchen staff, "Do as he wills,"
he nodded toward the empty water jars.

How He Came to Speak in Parables

The first time was a whim. Growing annoyed
at his repeated failure to get through,
he scanned his listless audience, and toyed
with likening the unknown to what they knew:
a brother's envy, taxes, mustard seed,
the way one ploughs a field or tends a herd.
Watching their rapt expressions, he perceived
how spirits, through the senses, could be stirred.
Their careworn lives made vivid, people yearned
to grasp the truth behind a homespun scene.
His teaching until now had been unleavened
by that essential germ. But he soon learned
from all the eager talk of what things mean,
how ample mystery was—like bread from heaven.

Brother James

The day we came to tell him Father died,
the crowd stood arm in arm; we couldn't get through.
My brothers shook their heads as they withdrew,
while I hung back. His ministry defied
all logic: its account of how God loves
put misfits first, brought monarchs to their knees.
His sayings branched out into mysteries
for thoughts to nestle in, like winded doves.
It made me think of how we'd played together
as children. He could take a tradesman's sons
and turn us into fierce centurions
with crockery and a plume of rooster feathers.
I loved him for it. How could it be sin
to conjure freedom from the hell you're in?

Legion

Jesus then asked him, "What is your name?" He said, "Legion";
for many demons had entered him.

(Luke 8:30, NRSV)

Enough of the cramped barrack! Let's explore
regions we haven't tried. This desert whets
a spirit's frothing appetite for more.
Let's rummage the interior, hurl threats
at the unwilling host—make him our slave—
and snarl and strut and curse and rack up debts
until he's driven howling to the grave!
Let's fill his wife and daughters with regrets.

Who calls on us? Why can't he let us be?
Does no one understand how hot it gets?
Look where the swineherd prods his infantry
of pigs: let's take possession of the pets
and charge them straight into the sea
to slosh our sweaty loins. Ah yes, let's. Let's!

The Cleansing of Mary Magdalene

He'd heard about a girl from Galilee,
who cried in bed and swore she had no rest
from hungry demons quarreling in her breast.
So he paid a visit. Crouching on one knee
and waving off her fractious family,
he asked each demon's name. Sternly he blessed
the things in her which could not be expressed
without trembling. This was the therapy
she needed to traverse her own Red Sea.

The next day she slept late; she bathed and dressed
and offered to escort her parents' guest
down to the gate. Reaching the cedar tree,
she looked back, frightened—then heard him say, "Come"
and walked beside him to Jerusalem.

Martha in the Kitchen

"Lord, do you not care that my sister has left me to do all the work by myself?"
(Luke 10:40, NRSV)

He shows up with his friends—like it's no trouble
to feed a dozen. What else can I do
but fill the pots and wait for them to bubble
while butchering a carcass for the stew?
I mince the herbs; I mash the roots; I stretch
moist dough; I pluck a fowl to glaze with mustard.
And while that cooks, I sweep the floors—then fetch
a brush to scrub the table down, all flustered.
That's when I see her lounging at his feet.
My blood boils! But what hits me like a rock
is how he says my worrying can't compete
with Mary's way of grazing among the flock.
Fine, I say to myself: why don't we eat
her tenderness? That fits in one small crock.

Simon's New Name

"And I tell you, you are Peter, and on this rock I will build my church . . ."

(Matt 16:18, NRSV)

Why me? Of all the sons in Palestine
who've joined his cause, leaving behind their kin,
why is the founder's privilege to be mine?
Disciples should be known for discipline,
whereas I've skipped through life awash in doubt.
How can he count on such a . . . stumbling block
to open Heaven's gate—or figure out
how best to spread the gospel to his flock?

On days our nets rise empty from the lake,
he'll smile, insisting each must eat his fill—
as though a man finds strength to undertake
more difficult conversions of the will
by having the audacity to make
himself firm first—his purpose, firmer still.

News from the Mount

Some of us stood in the sun, some under tents,
listening to the prophet as he stressed
how we—"salt of the earth"—were God's most blessed.
The more we heard, the more his words made sense.
His "kingdom" stirred up feelings so immense—
as if he were a bridegroom, we the guests
feasting on a prospective happiness
for which our royal host spared no expense.

By twilight we were ambling back to town.
The crickets' churr was drowned out by the hum
of thoughts we could not fully comprehend.
It seemed our lives had been turned upside down,
that night was dawn—a sparkling world to come
eclipsing our dull sands. To that, Amen.

The Pharisee's Quandary

He sounds convinced, but what if this is all
a fever? Aren't distempers of the brain
vented through dreams: so real, so beautiful,
the dreamer doesn't know he's gone insane?
He reasons from beliefs which have no cause;
his riddles, like the taunts of a coquette,
stump our priesthood. Seldom at a loss
for words sewn light as gossamer, his net
of paradox confounds us. May the fiend
who meddles in our Creator's steadfast plan
not tempt us with such speech, nor contravene
the ancient laws. Why listen to a man
whose mind is like a doorway to the sea?
Why drown oneself in his infinity?

Stoning an Adulteress

He knew too well the gossip of these men
who forced the woman, pleading, to her knees.
So when they tried to get him to condemn
her sin, he thought instead of how their lusts
would bubble up through hushed obscenities.
Stooping to press his finger in the dust,
he wrote the charge as custom had decreed.
"Let him," he cautioned, "who is free of sin
be first to throw a stone." Like onionskin
the men's cause shriveled. Foiled in their pride,
they fled from the tribunal in chagrin.
The woman, stunned, was of the lowest rank
and could not read the charge he had inscribed:
the broken law; her name; the space left blank.

Lazarus Among Friends

The last thing I remember is the wind
catching the sill, as Mary screamed my name—
and thinking it was better to give in
since nothing could be helped. Then numbness came.
How can I describe what happened next?
I vanished from myself; I showed no trace
of being in my corpse, which was unflexed
and shuttled to a cool, secluded space.
Not till I felt a prickling in my skin
and recognized his voice, calling my name,
did I begin to wonder where I'd been.
"Come out," he said. And like a child I came
forth in my linens. Such a cry was raised
that no one noticed: he looked just as dazed.

Herod's Banquet

A birthday gift: the sweaty, balding king
watching his daughter dance. Her half-veiled breast
intoxicates him. Belching, he suggests
she choose a prize. He pledges, "Anything."

Aware that her mother takes this as a sting,
Salome asks for her guidance—as though pressed
to make up for the failing of some test.

The mother answers firmly, "Tell him, bring
the baptist's head." With these words she defies
a husband who must now appreciate
how passion twists and flails before it dies.

Her daughter hoists the remnant of her hate:
the uninvited guest, whose downcast eyes
see nothing in a polished silver plate.

Transfiguration

He led us up the mountain's tufted ridge
to a plateau, where we were taught to curb
our hunger—chewing sprigs of potent herb.
The sun's beams slanted toward us like a bridge
into the furling clouds, whose bluish foam
enveloped him. We prayed. The landscape bloomed
with shadows, as his countenance assumed
a lunar sheen that lit the sky's grey dome.
Then voices bellowed through a pelting rain:
Elijah, Moses—seers who could be heard
communing with him in the crackling Word
which threatened to engulf the Lord's domain.

At dawn, with mouths still dry and vision blurred,
we made our slow descent back to the plain.

The Moneychanger

It must have been the doves that set him off.
Seeing them caged, he kicked the breeder's chair
so hard it knocked against a drover's trough
and sent goats scrambling through the crowded square.
He flipped the tables where our coins were weighed—
buckets of shekels chiming in midair!—
and tore the awnings off the colonnade,
screaming that we'd made this house of prayer
a den of thieves. With that, his fury ceased.
He looked at us—as if he'd seen despair—
and wandered out before the Temple priests
could flag down a patrolling legionnaire.
To cut the tension, someone raised a broom.
We laughed until the counting had resumed.

Lost Canticle of Mary Magdalene

He stirs the wind that teaches me to breathe;
He steers the dove, who trains my earthbound eye
to fasten on her errands through the sky.
In Him the crops and tides and seasons weave;
flood comes to chasten, rainfall to relieve
dry fields, upon whose nutrients all rely.
Over the precincts where men sell and buy

there hangs a patient sword: His to unsheathe
in glory at the last day—and with one blow
sever the brokers from their coin and clay.
His reckoning will lay bare what they owe;
His treasury of mercy shall repay
the humble—that their creditors may know
the value of the life He gives away.

The Disciple Whom Jesus Loved

... he was the one who had reclined next to Jesus at the supper and had said, "Lord, who is it that is going to betray you?"

(John 21:20, NRSV)

The others knew him spiritually, while I
adored him as a man: how his voice fluttered
when paying tribute to his aging mother;
the way he'd stop to listen; how his sighs
tempered the laughter fading from his eyes.
I'd take his arm to walk up steep, waved sand
and note the hints of tension in his hand.
He tried to warn us how a savior dies
for love; and still, it took me by surprise
the night he poured the wine and rinsed our feet,
and tore the bread and told us we would meet
in a better world. Their agony gave rise
to memoirs—gospels meant to spread his fame.
I made them promise not to use my name.

Gethsemane

"My Father, if it is possible, let this cup pass from me ..."
(Matt 26:39, NRSV)

Beneath the moon's warm glow, the trees look black.
A salt breeze sways the boughs, whose bristles grow
into a canopy. Here is no lack
of shelter—proof that what we yield, we owe.
While others sleep, I'll watch and be the weigher
of sorrow, weeder of a narrow track
that bends toward the kiss of a betrayer.
It's frightening, the expanse: the gulf my soul
must cross before I come to Your far stair.
Yet even as I hover on its brink,
soothed with the breath of olive flowers, I know
my flesh is weak. O Father, let me think
no more of what I do than to glance back
at this bewitching world. And take my drink.

The Man Who Would Be King

And they began saluting him, "Hail, King of the Jews!"
(Mark 15:18, NRSV)

He asked for it—by preaching he'd sit high
beside the Father, sorting sheep from goats
and doling out each soul's allotted payment.
Imagine: him we'd come to crucify
thinking such pompous horseshit wouldn't goad us!
We gave him what he wanted—royal raiment
made from a beggar's stinking purple tunic
and coils of prickly briar. In his right hand
we placed a reed, knelt down, read holy writ;
then snapped the scepter, flogged him like a eunuch.
By then he knew whose side was in command.
He stumbled up the pathway, glazed in spit—
anointed for his throne of tethered wood
almost as he'd predicted. That felt good.

Mary Magdalene Squares the Gospels

Mary Magdalene went and announced to the disciples, "I have seen the Lord" ...
(John 20:18, NRSV)

Line up the four accounts: no two agree
on what was uttered from the tomb, who heard,
how many white-garbed angels could be seen
sitting or standing, whether He appeared.
They clash because the men refused to trust
our testimony. Sneering at our "murmurs,"
each strove to make the story more robust—
spicing the facts with palatable rumors.
Only a woman fully understands
such wizardry. The words put in her mouth
show how a muffled past is stamped with man's
emboldened imprint. Now for the plain truth:
on a dark Sunday morning, working alone,
three women leaned their weight against one stone ...

The Fate of Judas

"... not one of them was lost except the one destined to be lost, so that the scripture might be fulfilled."

(John 17:12, NRSV)

He knew my faults as if they were his own:
my fondness for a bet, my secrecy.
The night we asked him which of us was prone
to give him up, his eyes were fixed on me.
I'm one of the diseased who do not change;
who promise to reform, yet come to grief—
pretending all we want is to exchange
our slow death for a martyr's swift relief.

Some say I've died. Although I can't divulge
my whereabouts, I've bought up half an acre.
My bed conceals an awkward silver bulge.
The other day I told the census taker,
"Christian." Why not? Without the likes of me,
his tortured faith would hold no poetry.

Mary's Assumption

She liked to wander—lost in thought, alone—
among the crags in Golgotha's blank face,
and find a nook within the eyeless stone
to rest an hour. From her hiding place
the world looked different: greener, trimmed with hope.
That very morning, strangers clutched her hem
to tell her his instruction helped them cope.
His legacy, she felt, would live in them.

Yet as she probed the mystery of his pain,
there lingered, faint as teardrops on a scroll,
the memory of a watchful boy's disdain
for ways of nature no one could control.

Her hands grew numb. She huddled from the wind,
trusting someone would come to take her in.

Epilogue

He thought he heard a voice—was it his own?—
asking the Father, *Why?* But as its rasp
receded in a low, deep-chested groan,
the silence took his breath. Between each gasp
his lips were dabbed with hyssop drenched in wine,
to numb the pain and ransom his faint spirit.
Who were these massed recruits of the divine
reviving him? Determined they should hear it,
he grunted, "It is finished."
                        Thus distilled,
his tremor of achievement came and went.
Beyond all striving, as the Father willed,
to demonstrate his empathy's extent,
a kingdom was in view—with passion spent
and words made flesh; a covenant fulfilled.

www.ingramcontent.com/pod-product-compliance
Lightning Source LLC
Chambersburg PA
CBHW051050030426
42339CB00006B/279